A BOOK OF
PROVERBS

*God's Wisdom for
Today's World*

RUTH BILLINGSLEY

XULON PRESS

Xulon Press
2301 Lucien Way #415
Maitland, FL 32751
407.339.4217
www.xulonpress.com

Paperback ISBN-13: 978-1-6312-9668-0
Ebook ISBN-13: 978-1-6312-9669-7

A BOOK OF
PROVERBS

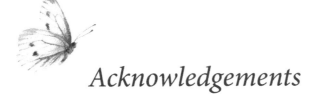

Acknowledgements

With deepest gratitude to:

God, for guiding me in every word

My husband, Bob, for his encouragement, support, and advice

Table of Contents

Introduction

The Book of Proverbs is God's wisdom for today's world. Even though written 3,000 years ago, His Word still speaks to us and gives advice through His eternal truths. We live in a world where we battle every day to make right choices. The world tells us one thing, and God's Word tells us another. We are caught in the middle! The storms of life come, and confusion is all around us. How do we live without being blown away? Do we stand out in the midst of danger, getting soaking wet, or do we grab an umbrella for shelter? One umbrella is the book of Proverbs, God's direction and guidance for all mankind. It is our protection as we seek to know the truth through the storms. Is your life full of hopes and dreams for the future? God wants you to accomplish them by trusting that His way, His counsel, is the path to a fulfilled and happy life. The decisions we make, the values we cherish, and the goals we want to reach are fundamental to who we are and how we fit into this vast universe. Proverbs is God's invitation to come, get under His umbrella, and be safe from the storm.

Proverbs is a collection of wise sayings and instructions, each one a statement of truth that questions man's values, moral behavior, the meaning of life, and right conduct. The two main principles that guide us are "The fear of God is the beginning of wisdom" (1:7, 9:10) and "Trust in the Lord with all your heart" (3:15). Its purpose is to teach wisdom that leads to a joy-filled and productive life, a life that honors and respects God. It can help in our work, with money, marriage, friendships, family life, and our relationship with God. This timeless book includes warnings and curses, as well as encouragement and blessings.

A Book of Proverbs is my interpretation of each proverb, written in poetic form. May these truths give you guidance that builds godly character in your life and be a reminder of how important making good choices can be. Following good advice leads to honesty, kindness, forgiveness, and humility, just to name a few. Take the time to meditate on these truths, and may God bless you as you apply God's Word in your daily life. Be safe from the storm.

> *"Understand these proverbs; interpret each word.*
> *They are good and holy; true benefits secured."*
> *Proverbs 1:6*

I pray you will be guided by God's truths in *A Book of Proverbs*.

Ruth Billingsley

Ingredients for Wisdom

The proverbs of Solomon, David was his father,
King of all Israel, wisdom's gifted author.

Wisdom and instruction, know them and understand.
Have justice and judgment; be fair to every man.

May the simple be prudent, the young man analyze.
Hear and increase learning; attain counsel that's wise.

Understand these proverbs; interpret each word.
They are good and holy, true benefits secured.

The fear of the Lord brings me to first recognize
All knowledge and wisdom, but fools hate and despise.

Obedience

Listen to me, my son, to instructions I give.
And your mother's teaching, it will help you to live.

These words will be a garland to grace around your head,
And chains about your neck show by honor you are led.

Good Company

If sinners entice you, do not give in to them.
If they say, "Come with us; we will kill; we'll condemn.

We will find possessions and fill our homes with loot.
Cast your lot among us. We'll share in this pursuit."

Son, do not walk with them. Keep away from their path.
Their feet run to evil. They shed blood in their wrath.

In vain, the net is spread; the innocent are sought.
Men lie in wait for others, but their own souls are caught.

Such is the end of those who are greedy for gain.
It takes away their lives; only truth will remain.

Listen to Wisdom

Wisdom calls aloud to all in the gates of the city.
She speaks to all who hear, "The simple, I'll pity.

Respond to my rebuke. I pour out my heart to you.
As I make my words known, I called, but you withdrew.

You rejected my hand, ignored my advice,
Dismissed my rebuke, so I'll refuse to be nice.

I'll laugh at your hardships; I'll mock when terror comes,
Turn my back on your storms; and when all is burdensome,

Then you will call on me; no answer will I give.
They will look for me, not finding where I live.

Since they hated knowledge and do not fear the Lord,
They will now eat the fruit of their schemes so abhorred.

Man's folly will kill him. Arrogance will destroy,
But whoever listens will be secure in joy."

Benefits of Wisdom

ACCEPT MY WORDS AND STORE THEM UP.

Benefits of Wisdom

My son, accept my words and store them up as well.
Listen to my treasures, and wisdom will indwell.

A Good Heart

Apply your heart to be understanding and kind.
Call out for more insight; cry out for a wise mind.

Look for her as silver, as for hidden treasure;
Then you will understand and fear with good measure.

The Lord gives wisdom. His mouth gives advice to all.
His words are for the upright. He is a shield when they call.

He will guard paths of justice, preserve the way of saints.
Hear and you'll understand righteousness and restraint.

Protection

When wisdom enters in, into your heart and soul,
Common sense will keep you sheltered in God's control.

It keeps you from evil, from men who speak bad things,
Who leave the paths of light to walk where darkness stings.

They rejoice in evil, delight in wicked wrath;
Their ways are crooked, and scheming is their path.

But wisdom delivers you from immoral women,
Who seduce and flatter with the lies that are given.

She forsakes all her friends. God's laws she doesn't learn.
Her house leads down to death; those who go don't return.

Walk in the way of goodness and keep righteousness near.
The upright and blameless will remain without fear.

But the wicked will be cut off from all the earth,
And the unfaithful ones will be exiled, no worth.

PROVERBS 3
Lessons of Wisdom

God's Laws

Do not forget My laws for then you will have peace.
Keep My commands within, and your days will increase.

Let not mercy and truth forsake you or depart.
Bind them around your neck; write them within your heart.

Then you will find favor, high esteem, and respect
In the sight of the Lord and to all men reflect.

Trust

Trust in the Lord your God; trust Him with all your heart.
Lean not on your own strength but on God from the start.

Acknowledge Him; submit to God in all your ways.
He will direct your paths, guide you through all your days.

Do not be wise or smart in your own self or eyes.
Fear the Lord and depart from evil, shame, and lies.

It will be health to you, strength and might to your bones.
You will then understand God controls all unknowns.

Honor

Honor the Lord with all that you have, you possess,
With all of your produce, and then you will be blessed.

So your barns will be filled with all kinds of good food.
Your vats will overflow with new wine to include.

My son, do not despise the Lord's chastening voice
Nor detest correction, but instead, now rejoice.

For God loves but corrects, just as a father would
Who delights in his son and helps him, as he should.

Now happy is the man who finds wisdom and gains
Understanding of My words; much profit he'll obtain.

Wisdom's proceeds are better than silver and gold,
More precious than rubies, better than all you hold.

All the things you desire cannot compare to her.
She holds your length of days; in her, riches occur.

All her ways are pleasant, and all her paths are peace.
She is a tree of life; hold on and don't release.

The Lord founded the earth, the heavens by His hands.
The depths were broken up; clouds drop, and dew expands.

This, all by His wisdom, the earth obeys His call.
By His understanding, He established it all.

Keep wisdom and good sense; retain them in your sight.
They are life to your soul and grace that shines bright.

Then you will walk safely, never stumbling feet.
You'll lie down unafraid, and your sleep will be sweet.

Don't fear sudden terror or trouble when it's near.
The Lord will be your help and keep your walk sincere.

Kindness

Do not withhold good from those to whom it is due.
When it is in your power, your hand will see them through.

Don't say to your neighbor, "Go and come back again.
Tomorrow I will give," but you had it. That's sin.

Do not devise evil with your neighbor or friend
For he dwells beside you, for safety's sake depend.

Do not strive with a man if he has done no harm.
Be at peace with all men; keep calm and don't alarm.

Don't envy the tyrant or choose any of his ways
For the perverse person will be cursed all his days.

The Lord's secret counsel is with the upright man.
He blesses his household over all his lifespan.

He will shun the scornful but gives grace to the humble.
The wise will have glory, but the fool will stumble.

Promises of Wisdom

HEAR, MY PRECIOUS CHILDREN.

Promises of Wisdom

Father's Words

Hear, my precious children, as your father preaches
And know good doctrine that understanding teaches.

I was my father's son, tender and young in years.
He taught me, and he said, "Retain my words; keep near.

Keep my commands and live. Get wisdom; understand.
Do not forget my words or forsake God's demands.

Wisdom will preserve you; if you love her, obey.
She will keep and protect. Exalt her every day.

Then she will promote you; your honor, she will sing.
Embrace her; receive grace. A crown of glory, she'll bring."

Hear, my son; receive my words. Your years will be complete.
I have taught you wisdom, leading down each path you meet.

Right Paths

When you walk down right paths, your steps won't be delayed.
When you run, you'll not fall; you will not be afraid.

Take hold of instruction; don't let it go in strife.
Keep her close beside you for she is your whole life.

Do not enter the path of any wicked men.
Avoid it and pass on; turn away from all sin.

They do not sleep unless they have done evil deeds
And have made someone fall for their hatred succeeds.

The path of righteousness is like the shining sun
That shines ever brighter. The perfect day is done.

The path of the wicked is like the dark, the deep.
They do not know what makes them stumble when they leap.

Right Heart

Give attention to my words. Do not let them depart
Not ever from your sight and keep them in your heart.

For they are life to those who find them and obey,
Health to a man's body, so listen to what I say.

Put away a lying mouth. Put wicked lips far from you.
Let your eyes look ahead; ponder the path you view.

Establish all your ways. Do not turn left or right.
Remove your foot from evil. Walk only in the light.

Pitfalls of Sin

Pay attention, my son. Hear wisdom; observe.
Learn my understanding, discretion to preserve.

Sinful Women

Your lips may keep knowledge—sinful women, not so.
They drip honey, so sweet. Their lips, like oil, flow.

In the end, they're bitter, sharp as a two-edged sword.
Their feet go down to death, and hell is their reward.

Ponder that road of life, so unstable, unsure.
Do not walk this pathway; hear me and remain pure.

Remove your way from her and from her open door.
You'll give your honor away, your years much to deplore.

Others will have your wealth and all you have worked for.
You will groan at the end when your body is no more.

You say, "Guidance, I hate. My life has not improved.
I hear my teacher's voice, but I will not be moved."

Honor Marriage

Drink from your own cistern; to your own wife, be true.
Marriage is to be blessed with honor and virtue.

For the ways of man God sees, and He ponders.
The wicked will be trapped; in sin, he wanders.

Roaming, lost, and confused, instruction given in vain,
His folly will be fatal; only death will remain.

Pitfalls of Folly
GO TO THE ANT; WATCH ITS WAYS.

PROVERBS 6
Pitfalls of Folly

Promises Broken

Be careful when you can pay a debt for a friend,
Shaking hands with a stranger, snared by words you send.

Deliver yourself from this. Go and be humble.
Plead to be free and resist sleep, lest you stumble.

If not, you will be like a gazelle that's hunted
Or a bird that's captured. Escape when confronted.

Lessons from the Ant

Go to the ant, you sluggard; watch its ways; be wise.
It has no overseer yet can organize.

It provides supplies during the warm summer time
And gathers food once again when harvest is prime.

How long will you slumber? When will you rise from sleep?
If you continue in ease, poverty you'll reap.

Wicked Man

A worthless, wicked man will walk around and lie.
He winks, drags his feet, and points fingers to defy.

Deceit is in his heart; sowing discord, his way.
Evil he plots daily, but soon comes judgment day.

These things the Lord hates: a proud look, a lying man,
Hands that shed innocent blood, hearts with a wicked plan,

Feet that run to evil, a false witness who lies,
And someone sowing discord when his brother cries.

Adultery

Keep your father's rules. Your mother's teachings endure.
Bind them on your heart and around your neck secure.

When you walk, they'll lead, and when you sleep, they'll keep you.
When awake, they will speak. Their words will see you through.

For these commands are a lamp, the lessons, a light.
These pathways of life will keep you from evil's plight.

Stay away from a harlot and each charming word.
Don't lust after beauty. Remember what you've heard.

Man becomes a crust of bread, and his life is turned.
Can a man come close to fire without his clothes burned?

Can one walk on hot coals without his feet seared?
So is he who's unfaithful; his outcome is feared.

A starving man will steal his food to satisfy,
Yet when he is caught, sevenfold he must supply.

Those who commit adultery do not understand.
They destroy their life. Shame and dishonor will command.

For jealousy will awaken a husband's wrath.
He shows no mercy; he walks down revenge's path.

He will not take payment and will refuse a bribe.
However great it is, he will cast it aside.

PROVERBS 7
Lessons on Morals

Son, keep my words within you; my commands, seek to apply;
Then you will live for my law is the apple of your eye.

Bind them upon your fingers and write each one on your heart.
My wisdom is your sister, understanding to impart.

They will sustain your morals, safe from all flattering words,
Away from the path of sin and enticing voices heard.

A harlot's ways are crafty, and her rebellion defies.
Her feet will always wander as she lurks in dark disguise.

She seeks out the foolish man; with alluring speech, he's sought.
She prepares her wicked web, and into it, he is caught.

With shameless face, she says, "I have peace offerings with me.
Today I have paid my vows, so come with me now, I plea.

I have prepared my chamber. Come to me, I now beseech.
My husband is not at home." And then he yields to her speech.

Now, with her flattering lips, his fall and disgrace will show
As he follows like an ox; to the slaughter, he will go.

As a deer steps in a noose and a bird into a snare,
He never knew the cost; his life was the payment to bear.

Now, therefore, listen to me; pay attention to my words.
Don't let your heart turn aside to her path with death assured.

She has cast down the wounded. Those slain were strong.
Her house is the way to hell; descending to death is wrong.

Remember my words, my son; keep them close to your heart.
You will be saved from pitfalls. Run from sin and be smart.

Aspects of Wisdom

EVERY PATH IS A CHOICE

Aspects of Wisdom

The Call of Wisdom

Does not wisdom cry out as she raises her voice?
She takes her stand on high. Every path is a choice.

She calls out to all men, to fools and simple ones.
Understand. Be cautious. Listen to me, my sons.

What I say is worthy. My lips speak what is right.
My mouth voices truth; deception is out of sight.

All of my words are just, not crooked or perverse.
They are simple and clear. Righteousness, they disperse.

Wisdom's Value

Receive my instruction more than silver or gold
For knowledge and wisdom have value to behold.

All things one may desire cannot compare to her
For wisdom surpasses what the world will prefer.

I, wisdom, have prudence, great knowledge, and foresight.
Show the fear of the Lord, hate evil, and seek what's right.

Counsel and strength are mine, and by me, kings will reign.
Rulers decree justice; princes rule and ordain.

I love those who love me and those who seek and find.
My riches and honor endure for all mankind.

My fruit, finer than gold, is better than silver too.
Those who love me receive treasures that will accrue.

Wisdom's Birth

The Lord possessed me from the dawning of time
Before His works of old for His plans are sublime.

When there were no oceans, I was given new birth.
When there were no fountains, I filled water on earth.

Before mountains were formed, before the hills were laid,
Before the fields or dust, I was brought forth and made.

I was there when He set the heavens in their place,
When He drew a circle and the deep had a face,

When He made clouds above and fixed the fountains deep,
Limited the waters so His command they'll keep,

When He marked out the earth, beside Him I would stay.
He's a master craftsman; I'm His delight each day.

I would always rejoice before Him and His word.
Now man is in the world. Will they obey what's heard?

Wisdom's Blessing

For blessed are those who keep my ways and wait to see,
Watching my doors daily and waiting just for me.

The Lord's life and favor will be what they will find,
But he who sins is wrong. Hate me, be left behind.

PROVERBS 9

Houses of Wisdom and Folly

Wisdom's Food

Wisdom has built her house with seven pillars, shaped.
Prepared with meat and wine, her table set and draped.

She has sent out her maids, and she calls from on high,
"Come, all who are simple. My wisdom you'll deny?

Come, eat my bread, my food. I've mixed a drink of wine.
Leave all your simple ways, and you will walk in line."

Wisdom's Correction

Correcting a mocker invites insult and pain.
Scolding a wicked man brings abuse and disdain.

Rebuking a wise man will bring love and goodwill.
Instructing a wise man will make him wiser still.

Teaching a righteous man makes learning increase
For the fear of the Lord begins wisdom's release.

The knowledge of the Lord understands truth.
Your days will be many, life added to your youth.

Wisdom will reward you when your knowledge is known.
If you are a mocker, you will suffer alone.

Folly Compared

Folly is a woman who is simple and loud.
She sits at her front door on a seat high and proud.

She calls to those who pass, who go straight on their way.
The simple turn in here, and this is what she'll say,

"Stolen water is sweet. Bread in secret is fine.
It's delicious and good. Come and see what is mine."

But little do they know that many dead are there,
And her guests are down deep in the depths of despair.

The Complaint

7 To execute vengeance upon the heathen, *and* punishments upon the people;

8 To bind their kings with chains, and their nobles with fetters of iron;

9 To execute upon them the judgment written: this honour have all his saints. Praise ye the LORD.

PSALM 150

Praise ye the LORD. Praise God in his sanctuary: praise him in the firmament of his power.

2 Praise him for his mighty acts: praise him according to his excellent greatness.

3 Praise him with the sound of the trumpet: praise him with the psaltery and harp.

4 Praise him with the timbrel and dance: praise him with stringed instruments and organs.

5 Praise him upon the loud cymbals: praise him upon the high sounding cymbals.

6 Let every thing that hath breath praise the LORD. Praise

THE PROVERBS

CHAPTER 1

THE proverbs of Sŏl'o-mon the son of Dā'vid, king of Ĭs'ra-el;

2 To know wisdom and instruction; to perceive the words of understanding;

3 To receive the instruction of wisdom, justice, and judgment, and equity;

4 To give subtilty to the simple, to the young man knowledge and discretion.

5 A wise *man* will hear, and will increase learning; and a man of understanding shall attain unto wise counsels:

6 To understand a proverb, and the interpretation; the words of the wise, and their dark sayings.

7 The fear of the LORD *is* the beginning of knowledge: *but* fools despise wisdom and instruction.

16 For their feet run to evil, and make haste to shed blood.

17 Surely in vain the net is spread in the sight of any bird.

18 And they lay wait for their *own* blood; they lurk privily for their *own* lives.

19 So *are* the ways of every one that is greedy of gain; *which* taketh away the life of the owners thereof.

20 ¶ Wisdom crieth without; she uttereth her voice in the streets:

21 She crieth in the chief place of concourse, in the openings of the gates: in the city she uttereth her words, *saying*,

22 How long, ye simple ones, will ye love simplicity? and the scorners delight in their scorning, and fools hate knowledge?

23 Turn you at my reproof: behold, I will pour out my spirit unto you, I will make known my words unto you.

24 Because I have called, and ye refused; I have stretched out my hand, and no man regarded;

25 But ye have set at nought all my counsel, and would none of my reproof:

26 I also will

Proverbs of Solomon
THE RIGHTEOUS SOUL THE LORD FEEDS.

PROVERBS 10
Proverbs of Solomon

An Honest Life

A wise son brings his father joy, but a foolish one brings grief.
Building wealth profits nothing, but righteousness will bring relief.

The righteous soul the Lord feeds, but the wicked's desire is lost.
Lazy hands make a man poor, but diligent ones know the cost.

Reaping in summer is wise, but sleeping at harvest is shame.
Blessings crown the righteous, but violence will not proclaim.

A good man's memories are blessed; a wicked man's name will rot.
The wise in heart accept commands; a chattering fool will not.

He who has integrity walks securely and unshaken,
But he who takes crooked paths will be found out and forsaken.

He whose eye winks causes grief. A fool's tongue causes ruin.
Righteous words are life's fountain. Evil ones have trouble brewin.'

Hatred stirs up worry and strife, but love covers all sin.
Wisdom is on clever lips, but the rod is for foolish men.

Wise men store up knowledge, but defeat is on a fool's lips.
Rich men's wealth is their focus, but the poor are in ruin's grips.

A Disciplined Life

The righteous' labor leads to life, but sin's wages always pay.
Keeping instruction leads to life. Shunning reproof leads astray.

Whoever hides hatred has lied; slander is spread by a fool.
When words are many, sin is there. Holding your tongue is the rule.

The words of the righteous are worth silver and will feed many.
Wicked men's hearts are worthless. Wisdom? They don't have any.

The blessings of the Lord bring wealth, with no trouble to admit.
A fool finds pleasure in evil, but a just man will submit.

The wicked are overtaken by what they fear will soon come,
But what the righteous man desires will be granted, every one.

When the great whirlwind passes by, the wicked are no more,
But the righteous are safe and sound. God's plan is an open door.

As vinegar is to the teeth and smoke is to the eyes,
So is a lazy messenger, who is sent but is not wise.

A God-Fearing Life

The fear of the Lord adds to life, but wicked men's years are cut short.
The hope of the righteous is joy, but evil has no support.

The way of the Lord is a refuge for the righteous and upright,
But it is the ruin of those who work to sin in the night.

The righteous will not be removed; the wicked will not survive.
A righteous mouth brings wisdom, but a corrupt one won't thrive.

The lips of the righteous will know what is fitting and fair,
But the mouth of the wicked man only leads to despair.

A Treasury of Knowledge

Good Direction

The Lord hates dishonest scales, but a just weight is His delight.
When pride comes, then comes disgrace, but the humble are right.

Honesty of a righteous man will direct him all his life.
The unfaithful are destroyed by their hypocrisy and strife.

Wealth is vain in wrath's day, but righteousness prevents death.
The blameless directs his way, but the wicked fall at each breath.

The upright will be saved by their righteousness and virtue,
But the unfaithful are trapped by evil desires that ensue.

When wicked men take their last breath, all their hopes will die.
Their power comes to nothing, and their lives never testify.

The righteous man will be rescued from his trouble and woes.
Sorrow comes on the wicked, so be wise; escape from all foes.

The godless destroys his neighbor with words of hate and lies,
But the righteous man escapes loss because he is wise.

When the righteous prospers, the city rejoices with praise.
When the wicked perish, shouts of joy and delight we'll raise.

Through the blessings of the upright, a city is lifted high,
But by the mouth of the wicked, it will be passed by.

A man who lacks judgment laughs at and insults his neighbor,
But a man of understanding is a friend maker.

A gossip betrays a secret; a tattle repeats each word.
But he, who is faithful, conceals everything that is heard.

Where there is no counsel, nations and the people will fall,
But with many advisors, it's victory and safety for all.

He who puts up security will surely suffer much,
But one who refuses him will be safe, not used as a crutch.

A gracious woman gains respect, but mean men gain only wealth.
A kind man benefits, but a cruel man may have poor health.

A God-Shaped Life

The wicked man earns false wages, but righteousness reaps gain.
The righteous man has life, but the evil man, death attains.

The Lord hates men of mean hearts but loves the blameless' ways.
All the wicked will be punished, but the righteous will be praised.

Like a gold ring in a pig's snout, so is a beautiful woman
Who shows no caution. She is lovely, but God will shun.

The desire of the righteous man ends in good and in grace,
But the hope of the wicked man ends in wrath's firm embrace.

One man gives freely yet gains; another withholds but is poor.
A generous man prospers; refreshing others gives him more.

People curse the man who hoards but bless him who will sell.
Seeking good finds favor, but trouble comes to those who rebel.

Whoever trusts in riches will never succeed but will fall,
But the righteous will thrive and grow like foliage, so tall.

He who troubles his family will inherit the wind,
And the foolish man will be a servant in the end.

The fruit of the righteous is a tree of freedom and life.
The one who wins souls is wise; he will have peace, not strife.

If the righteous receive their due on earth and seem secure,
How much more the ungodly for the fate of sinners is sure.

Man's Choices

THE HEART OF MAN LOVES KNOWLEDGE.

Man's Choices

The Heart of Man

The heart of man loves knowledge. Hate correction? That's absurd.
Obtain favor from the Lord for He condemns wicked words.

Wickedness brings great loss, but the righteous man stands firm.
Good wives are husbands' crowns, but their shame is like a worm.

Righteous men's plans are just, but wicked ones only condemn.
Their talk lies in wait for blood, but the upright's speech saves them.

Wicked men can be conquered, but the righteous stand strong.
A man's praised by his wisdom, but a corrupt mind is wrong.

Better to be nobody and have servants to help you
Than pretend to be esteemed and have no food to get through.

Righteous men love animals, but the wicked are cruel.
He who works his land has food, but fantasies chase a fool.

The wicked desire to steal, but the righteous yields much fruit.
Evil men sin with their talk, but righteous men flee dispute.

The fruit of man's lips are filled with good things, we are told.
His work will be his reward; it will pay a thousand-fold.

The Mind of Man

The way of a fool seems right, but a wise man heeds advice.
A fool will show his anger, but a sensible man will be nice.

A man who speaks truth is wise; a false witness has deceit.
Reckless words cut like a sword, but a wise tongue heals complete.

Truthful lips last forever, but a lying tongue has no time.
Deceitful hearts plot evil, but peace brings joy that's sublime.

No harm befalls the righteous, but the wicked? Every day.
The Lord detests lying lips, but He delights in truth's way.

A wise man keeps his knowledge, but folly is the fool's course.
The diligent hand will rule, but lazy men work by force.

An anxious heart is heavy, causing hopelessness and fright,
But a good word is cheerful; it fills the heart with delight.

Righteous men choose friends with care for some lead them wrong.
Lazy men refuse to cook, but workers will eat lifelong.

In righteousness, there is life, and its pathway has no death,
So heed the words of good men and have blessings at each breath.

PROVERBS 13

Walk with the Wise

Hate What is False

A wise son obeys instruction, but a mocker does not hear.
A man enjoys good things, but evil holds violence dear.

He who guards his words has life, but speaking rashly will fail.
The sluggard craves but gets nothing; the diligent will prevail.

The righteous hates what is false, but the wicked brings disgrace.
Righteousness guards integrity, but wickedness is sin's place.

One man pretends to have riches, and yet he has no portion.
Another pretends to be poor, but he has a great fortune.

A man's wealth may ransom his life, but a poor man has no doubt.
The light of the righteous shines bright. The wicked is snuffed out.

Hate What is Foolish

Pride breeds quarrels and dissention, but wisdom is found to last.
Dishonest money will dwindle, but saving will add up fast.

Abandoned hope makes the heart sick, but longings met are life.
He who scorns instruction will pay, but obeying reduces strife.

Wise instruction is life's fountain turning from death's regard.
Good understanding wins favor, but unfaithful ways are hard.

Hate What is Wrong

A wise man acts with knowledge, but fools show childish feelings.
A bad messenger makes trouble, but honesty brings healing.

Ignoring discipline brings shame, but heeding correction is great.
A wish fulfilled is sweet, but fools won't turn from evil's fate.

He who walks with wise men is wise, but a fool's friend will grieve.
Misfortune seeks the sinner, but prosperity helps those who believe.

Good men leave an inheritance for grandchildren who will come,
But a sinner's is stored up for the righteous. It's quite a sum.

A poor man's field may produce food, but injustice sweeps it away.
The righteous eat all they want, but the wicked hunger each day.

He who spares the rod hates his son, but he who loves has concern.
Showing discipline with love is the way to be caring yet stern.

The righteous eat to their heart's content until they are satisfied,
But the stomach of the wicked is hungry and empty inside.

The Choices Between Wisdom and Folly

SEE THE WAYS OF LIFE AND DEATH.

PROVERBS 14
The Choices Between Wisdom and Folly

The Ways of Life and Death

The wise woman builds her house, but the foolish tears hers apart.
He whose walk is right fears the Lord, but evil men have no heart.

A fool's talk is a rod of pride, but words of the wise will protect.
Where no oxen are, it is clean, but harvest brings the ox respect.

A faithful witness does not lie, but a false witness won't be true.
A scoffer seeks wisdom in vain, but the wise will have it in view.

Stay away from a foolish man; knowledge will not be on his lips.
The prudent gives thoughts to his ways, but the folly of fools tricks.

Fools mock at every wrong, but the good man, the upright employ.
The heart knows its bitterness, and no one else will share its joy.

The wicked man's house won't last, but the good, God will defend.
There is a way that seems right, but death's door will be at its end.

The Heart Knows

Even in joy and in laughter, the heart may have sorrow and grief.
The faithless pay for their way, but God gives the righteous relief.

The simple believe every word, but the wise considers his path.
He fears and departs from evil, but a fool is reckless with wrath.

A quick-tempered man acts foolish, and a crafty man is hated.
The simple inherit folly, but the prudent is educated.

Evil bows before the good and will also bow at the righteous gate.
Neighbors will shun the poor, but few will see the rich and hate.

Despising a neighbor is sin, but blessed is the man who is kind.
Devising evil leads astray, so be good, love and faithfulness find.

In all labor, there is profit, but idle talk sees poverty.
The wise have a crown of riches, but the fools will never be free.

Fear the Lord

A true witness delivers souls, but a false witness will tell lies.
He who fears the Lord is secure, and for his children, he provides.

The fear of the Lord brings life, turning men from death's snare.
A king's honor is in his people; without them, there's only despair.

Be Faithful and True

A patient man is slow to wrath. He understands and will forgive,
But he who has a quick temper, for folly and self he will live.

A heart at peace has life and health; our bodies react with delight.
But envy will crumble our bones; it is rottenness, causing blight.

He who oppresses the poor shows contempt for our God, indeed,
But he who honors our Maker will show mercy to those in need.

The wicked will be banished, but the righteous find home in death.
Wisdom's heart has insight, but a fool's fails with each breath.

The Lord is Watching

He Sees Evil and Good

A gentle answer turns away wrath, but a harsh word stirs up anger.
A wise tongue exalts knowledge, but a fool's mouth spews slander.

The Lord's eyes are everywhere; watching evil and good, His goal.
A healthy tongue is a tree of life, but a false tongue ruins the soul.

A fool shuns his father's advice, but he who is wise honors change.
Treasure is the house of the right, but great debt, wicked arrange.

He Sees Our Hearts

Wise lips disperse knowledge, but a fool's heart does not.
A wicked man's sacrifice is hated, but a good man's prayer is sought.

The Lord scorns the way of the wicked but loves the pure and wise.
Discipline awaits him who wanders. He who hates correction dies.

Death and destruction are before God; so are the hearts of men.
A mocker will resent correction; he will not ask advice, a sin.

A happy heart makes a joyful face, but the spirit falls with heartache.
The clever heart seeks knowledge, but the fool's folly will forsake.

Tragic are the days of the helpless, but the cheerful heart is a treat.
Better a little with fear of God than great wealth with defeat.

He Sees Our Choices

Better a meal of good vegetables where there is love and care
Than a dinner of a fattened calf with hatred that leads to warfare.

Hot-tempered men stir up quarrels, but patient men calm discord.
A lazy man's way has thorns, but the upright walks with the Lord.

A wise son brings joy to his father, but a fool will hate his mother.
Folly delights the undiscerning, but the wise walk like no other.

Without counsel, plans fail, but gain when advisors are heard.
Joy is found in smart replies, and how good is a timely word!

He Sees Our Paths

Life's pathway leads upward for the wise to keep him from hell.
The Lord ruins proud men's homes but guards where widows dwell.

The thoughts of the wicked are despised, but joy, the pure give.
A greedy man has family trouble, but he who hates bribes will live.

The heart of the righteous will answer with the study of each word,
But the mouth of the wicked gushes with evil, useless and absurd.

The Lord is far from the wicked, but good men's prayer, He owns.
Happiness is joy to the heart, and good news is health to the bones.

He Sees Our Humility

The ear that hears rebukes in life will be at home among the wise,
But he who shuts his ears to advise will be depressed; he'll agonize.

He who ignores any discipline despises himself and his soul,
But whoever follows correction gains understanding and control.

The fear of the Lord teaches wisdom, lessons to follow God's law.
Humility comes before honor, so look to each other with awe.

Concerning Life
and Conduct

TRUST IN THE LORD.

PROVERBS 16
Concerning Life and Conduct

Trust the Lord

Man plans from the heart, but from the Lord, answers are sent.
All man's ways seem pure to him, but the Lord sees his intent.

Commit to the Lord all you do, and all your plans will succeed.
The Lord controls all He has made, even the wicked man's deed.

The Lord detests the proud of heart; their punishment is sure.
Love and faithfulness atone sin; fear of the Lord keeps man pure.

When the ways of man please the Lord, enemies live in peace.
Better a little with fairness than injustice with much increase.

In his heart, a man plans his course, but his steps, the Lord directs.
The king's lips speak divination, and his mouth, betrayal reflects.

Trust Honesty

Honest weights and scales are the Lord's; He made them to endure.
A king detests all wrongdoing; his throne of righteousness, secure.

Kings take pleasure in honest lips; they value speaking what is right.
A king's fury conveys words of death, but a wise man is his delight.

Light in the king's face conveys life; his favor is like rain in spring.
Wisdom is better than gold and much more than silver can bring.

The highway of the upright man will stay far from evil and sin.
He who guards his way will shield his life without and within.

Trust Wisdom

Pride will go before destruction, a vain spirit before a fall.
Better to be lowly in heart than to be proud, then become small.

Whoever obeys instruction prospers and is blessed by the Lord.
The wise in heart are discerning, and pleasant words are their reward.

Understanding is a fountain; it will flow with life's benefit,
But folly brings on punishment to fools who will never commit.

A wise man's heart guides his mouth; to instruction, his lips appeal.
Pleasant words are a honeycomb, sweet to the soul, and bones heal.

There is a way that seems right but leads to death in the end.
The laborer works for himself for his hunger he must attend.

Trust Kindness

The ungodly digs up evil; it's on his lips like a hot fire.
A perverse man will harvest strife, and a gossip fills friends with ire.

A violent man will entice his neighbors away from good thoughts.
He winks his eye at perverse things, and his lips reveal evil plots.

Gray hair is a crown of splendor; it is gained by a righteous life.
Better a patient and kind man than a warrior who's full of strife.

A man who controls his temper is better than a soldier's plans.
The lot is cast into the lap, but results are in the Lord's hands.

Consequences of a Fool

A Fool's Speech

Better a dry bread crust with quiet and peace
Than a house of plenty that causes strife's increase.

A wise servant will rule over a shameful son.
He'll share in the birthright with the brothers, each one.

The pot refines silver; the furnace is for gold,
But the Lord will test hearts. What does every man's hold?

A wicked man listens to evil lips that speak.
A liar will notice malicious tongues that reek.

He who mocks the poor shows contempt for his Maker.
He who's glad at hardships is a vile lawbreaker.

Grandchildren are the crowns of the aged, of old men,
And parents are the pride of children, joy within.

A fool's excellent speech is arrogant and vain
And even seems much worse when lying just for gain.

A bribe is like a charm to the one who gives it.
Wherever he will turn, he'll succeed; he'll outwit.

He who covers over an offense promotes love,
But he who repeats words gives his close friends a shove.

Rebuke has more effect for a discerning man
Than one hundred lashes for fools with no plan.

A Fool's Actions

An evil man will seek rebellion and unrest,
So a cruel messenger will be sent to arrest.

Better to meet a bear that's been robbed of her cubs
Than a fool who's been caught in his foolish hubbub.

Rewarding evil when humble deeds have been done
Will bring outrage and shame to a house; scorn's begun.

Starting a harsh quarrel is like breaching a dam,
So drop any matter before causing a scam.

You'll acquit the guilty; the innocent, you'll blame.
The Lord detests them both, so be fair what you claim.

Of what use is money in the hand of a fool
Since he has no desire to be wise, just cruel?

A friend loves at all times. Friendship, a gift we gain.
A brother, born for grief, will help you with your pain.

A man who will shake hands in a pledge for a friend
Is lacking in judgment; misfortune may ascend.

He who loves to quarrel causes trouble, loves sin.
He who builds a high gate, destruction will come in.

A man of perverse heart will not prosper or thrive.
He whose tongue is lying uses tricks to survive.

A Foolish Son

Having a foolish son causes sadness and grief.
There is no joy or hope for his father's belief.

A cheerful, happy heart is good medicine, true,
But a broken spirit makes dry bones all askew.

A wicked, sinful man accepts a secret bribe.
He will pervert justice; to evil, he'll ascribe.

A discerning, good man keeps wisdom in his view,
But a fool's eyes wander the whole earth to pursue.

A foolish son brings grief to his father, such pain.
Bitterness and trouble are his mother's disdain.

It's not good to punish any innocent man
Or to flog officials when for justice they stand.

A man who has knowledge uses words with control.
Men of understanding will possess a calm soul.

Even a fool seems wise if he keeps his tongue mute.
And he seems discerning if he resists dispute.

Words of Death and Life

THE NAME OF THE LORD IS A STRONG, SAFE TOWER.

PROVERBS 18
Words of Death and Life

Selfish Words

An unfriendly man will pursue selfish ends,
And all sound judgment he will mock; he offends.

Fools find no pleasure in wisdom or insight,
But their opinions bring their own hearts delight.

When wickedness comes, then contempt comes also.
Shame will bring disgrace, and all things are brought low.

Words of a man's mouth are deep waters of woe,
But wisdom's fountain is a brook that will flow.

It is never good to give evil favors
Or see the righteous when all justice waivers.

Foolish Words

The lips of a fool bring him conflict and strife;
His mouth brings defeat when he speaks about life.

A fool's mouth brings grief; it's his failure and doom.
His lips are a snare and to his soul, a tomb.

A talebearer's words are like a tasty bite;
They go to the depth of a man's soul with might.

One who is lazy, who is slack in his work,
Is brother to him who destroys with a smirk.

The name of the Lord is a strong, safe tower;
The righteous find it sheltered by His power.

Humble Words

The wealth of the rich see their city secure,
And like a high wall, imagine it is sure.

Before his downfall, the heart of man is proud.
Humility comes before honor's allowed.

He who gives answers before he is aware
Brings folly and shame and to himself, a snare.

A man's spirit helps when he is sick and weak,
But a crushed spirit, who can bear since it's bleak?

The discerning heart acquires knowledge that's good.
The ears of the wise seek it out, as they should.

The gift of a man opens the door of fate
And brings him into the presence of the great.

Discerning Words

The first to present his case and cause seems right
'Til another comes and questions with insight.

Casting lots settles disputes, conflicts, and feuds
And keeps strong rivals apart for they'll intrude.

An offended brother is more unyielding and hard,
More than a walled city with soldiers that guard.

Disputes and quarrels are like a castle with bars,
Locking out brothers with hurtful wounds and scars.

With words, a man speaks. His stomach will be filled,
And his lips' harvest will satisfy and build.

The tongue has power over man's life and death,
And those who love it eat its fruit with each breath.

Loving Words

He who finds a wife finds what is good and right.
He receives favor from the Lord, such delight.

A poor man will plead for mercy, so humble,
But the rich answer harshly and will grumble.

Men with many friends may not trust another,
But there is a friend who is like a brother.

Listen and Learn

Learn Truth

Better a poor man who blamelessly walks
Than a fool whose lips are mean when he talks.

It is never good to have drive or zeal
Without knowing truth or grasp what is real.

A man's own folly will ruin his life
As his heart rages at the Lord with strife.

Wealth brings many friends, but a poor man? No.
Friends will desert him; alone, he's brought low.

A lying witness will not be set free.
Punishment for him will be the decree.

Learn Justice

Many want favor with the upper class
And are friends with men who give gifts in mass.

A poor man is shunned by all of his kin,
And also, his friends avoid him, such sin.

Though he pursues them with pleading profound,
They have disappeared, nowhere to be found.

He who gets wisdom will love his own soul.
Cherishing knowledge prospers with control.

Any false witness will be punished first;
He who pours out lies will perish, be cursed.

Learn Humility

It is not fitting for a fool to live
With riches and joy, not wanting to give.

Nor should a servant rule over a prince;
That would not be right and hard to convince.

Man's wisdom gives him patience and control.
He will glory since forgiveness is his goal.

A king's rage is like a lion's roar, alas,
But his good favor is like dew on grass.

A foolish, weak son ruins his father.
A quarrelsome wife is such a bother.

Houses and riches inherited all,
But a prudent wife answers the Lord's call.

Learn Control

Laziness causes sleep in solitude.
An idle person will hunger for food.

He who keeps the law keeps his soul and mind,
But if he's careless, he'll be left behind.

He who has pity on the poor and low
Lends to the Lord God; his reward will flow.

Discipline your son for then there is hope.
Do not set your heart on his downward slope.

A hot-tempered man must have discipline.
If you rescue him, you'll do it again.

Learn Trust

Accept instruction; listen to advice,
And then in the end, you'll be wise and nice.

Many are the plans in the heart of man,
But the Lord's purpose will always stand.

What a man desires is love until he dies.
Better to be poor than a man who lies.

The fear of the Lord leads to life, for sure.
Then one rests content, trouble to defer.

Learn to Regret

Lazy men, sluggards, will not themselves feed;
The Word before them they refuse to read.

Chastise a mocker; the simple will learn.
Rebuke a wise man; he'll humbly discern.

Robbing his father will bring a son shame.
Driving out his mother gives him a bad name.

Don't stop listening to teaching that's good.
Don't stray from wisdom, its words understood.

A corrupt witness at justice will jest.
A wicked man's mouth swallows evil's quest.

Judgments are prepared for those who break rules;
Beatings are prepared for the backs of fools.

Warnings

KEEP ALERT.

PROVERBS 20
Warnings

Keep Alert

Wine is a mocker, and beer will cause a brawl.
Those men led astray see foolishness befall.

The wrath of a king is like a lion's cry.
He who angers him forfeits life; he will die.

It's honorable to walk away from strife,
But every fool will quarrel all his life.

A sluggard won't plow in the winter season,
So at harvest time, he begs with good reason.

Counsel in man's heart is like water that's deep,
But understanding will draw it out to reap.

Most men will proclaim their love will never fail,
But a faithful man? You'll look to no avail.

The righteous man leads, integrity his quest.
His children follow and are happy and blessed.

When a king sits down on his throne to judge,
He scatters evil and sees every grudge.

Keep Pure

Who can ever say, "I have kept my heart pure.
I am clean and sinless." Can you be so sure?

Differing weights and measures that are askew,
The Lord hates them, so make sure they are true.

Even a small child will be known by his deeds,
Whether they are pure and righteousness succeeds.

Ears that can hear sounds, eyes that can see the earth,
The Lord has made both; praise Him of great worth.

Do not love sleep, or you will become poor.
Stay awake and see. You will have food for sure.

Keep Secure

"It's good for nothing," says the man who has bought,
But when he gets home, he boasts about what he got.

There are gold and rubies with ample renewals,
But lips that speak knowledge are precious jewels.

Take a stranger's clothes and use for a promised pledge,
And for a strange woman, be wise in what's alleged.

Food gained by deceit when consumed, will taste sweet,
But then end up with a mouth full of concrete.

Make your future plans by seeking good advice,
And if you wage war, have guidance to suffice.

Keep Good Words

A gossip reveals hidden secrets and such;
Therefore, stay away from those who talk too much.

Whoever curses his parents each day,
His lamp will be out, and deep darkness will stay.

An inheritance gained quickly at the start
Will never be blessed; at the end, it will depart.

Do not ever say, "I'll repay for this wrong!"
Just wait for the Lord; He will save you lifelong.

All dishonest scales and inconsistent weights
Do not please the Lord; a wrong practice, He hates.

The steps of a man the Lord will lead every day.
How then can a man understand his own way?

This is a man's trap; "It's holy," he will say,
And after his vows, see it was not God's way.

Keep the Faith

A wise king sifts out the wicked and unclean;
Like a threshing wheel, he winnows to glean.

The lamp of the Lord searches out a man's heart.
To a man's spirit, God's bright light will impart.

Honor and faithfulness will keep a king secure.
Through love, his throne will be made safe and sure.

The strength of young men is their glory and fame.
Gray hair of the old is their splendor and acclaim.

Blows and wounds will cleanse away evil's shame,
And beatings purge the depths of the heart's frame.

What are Your Motives?

Your Heart

The king's heart is in the Lord's hand. He directs it like a river.
It goes where He wishes, and His perfect plan will deliver.

All of man's ways seem right to him, but the Lord weighs the heart.
Righteousness is better than the sacrifices you impart.

Haughty eyes and proud hearts are the lamp of many wicked sins.
Good plans lead to profit, but haste is where poverty begins.

Fortune made by a lying tongue is a brief vapor, a snare.
Violence drags men from doing what's right; they do not care.

Your Sin

The guilty are devious, but an honest man is upright.
Better to live on a roof than with a wife who likes to fight.

The wicked man craves evil, and his neighbor gets no mercy.
He delights to do mischief and loves to have controversy.

When a mocker is punished, men take notice and become wise.
When a wise man is instructed, he sees God's truth arise.

The righteous God wisely considers the wicked man's lifestyle.
He will bring the house of those men to ruin, for they are vile.

He who shuts his ears to the cry of the poor will not be heard.
Gifts given in secret soothe anger. Bribes calm an angry word.

Your Justice

When justice is done, it brings great joy to all men who believe,
But to evildoers, terror and destruction they receive.

Any man who strays from the path of understanding God's Word
Will come to rest among the dead. He's deaf to what he has heard.

He who loves pleasure and wine will become poor, denying blame.
The wicked are ransom for the righteous. They'll be put to shame.

Better to live in a desert than with a wife who's quarrelsome.
Contention and anger will be hard for her to overcome.

There are food and oil stored up in the house of the wise man,
But a foolish man will quickly devour all that he can.

He who pursues righteousness will find life and honor and love.
Success and happiness come by the mercy of God above.

Wise men attack great cities, pulling down strongholds that men trust.
Wisdom is better than strength, giving victory to the just.

Your Words

He who guards his mouth and his tongue will try to avoid trouble.
The proud man, "Mocker," is his name; he brings his life to rubble.

The sluggard's desire is his death; he refuses to labor.
He covets all the day, but the righteous gives to his neighbor.

The sacrifice of the wicked is brought with evil intent.
A false witness will perish, but speaking the truth brings content.

A wicked man puts up a bold front; he is callous to guilt,
But an upright man is honest, and on God, his life is built.

Against the Lord God there is no wisdom, counsel, or reward.
The horse prepares for battle, but victory rests with the Lord.

Boundary Lines
THE EYES OF THE LORD KEEP WATCH.

Boundary Lines

A Good Name

A good name is to be chosen, rather than great wealth,
And loving favor, rather than silver or good health.

Rich and poor have this in common—the Lord made them all.
They help when working together, whatever befall.

A prudent man foresees danger and finds a safe place,
But the simple keep on going and suffer disgrace.

Humility, obedience, and fear of the Lord
Will bring wealth, honor, and life, a vast and great reward.

In the paths of a wicked man lie sharp thorns and snares,
But he who guards his soul keeps from pain and despair.

Train up a child in the right way, the way he should go,
And when he matures and is old, his wisdom will show.

A Good Attitude

The rich will rule over the poor, and this, too, is true:
The borrower will be servant when money is due.

He who sows iniquity's sin reaps sorrow in life.
The rod of his anger will fail among pain and strife.

He who has a generous eye will be blessed, divine,
For he provides bread to the poor; it's by God's design.

Drive out the mocker and his grief; then quarrels will end.
A man of pure heart and kind speech will be the king's friend.

The eyes of the Lord God keep watch over man's knowledge,
And He frustrates the hateful words of each faithless pledge.

The lazy sluggard may declare, "A lion's outside!"
Or, "I'll be murdered in the streets," so at home he'll hide.

The mouth of an adulteress is a deep, deep pit.
He who is under the Lord's wrath will fall into it.

Folly is bound up in the heart, even in a child,
But the strict rod of discipline will help him be mild.

He who oppresses a poor man so wealth will increase
And he who gives gifts to the rich will neither see peace.

30 Wise Sayings

Listen to sayings of the wise; pay attention, please.
Apply your heart to what I teach; keep each one of these.

Have them all ready on your lips; trust only the Lord.
I'll teach each of you today. It's all for your reward.

I've written sayings of counsel, sayings that are true.
They have knowledge and good insight and are just for you.

Teaching you reliable words that you will then know
To give sound and fitting answers and to others show.

#1 The Poor

Don't take advantage of the poor or crush the needy
For the Lord will take up their case and judge the seedy.

#2 Friends

Don't make friends with an angry man; he'll capture your soul.
Stay away from a hot-tempered person; do not go.

#3 Debts

Don't be one of those who shakes hands in a pledge or vow.
Don't use security for debts. God's plan, you allow.

If you lack any means to pay, everything you'll lose,
So do not be a borrower; be wise and refuse.

#4 Traditions

Don't remove the ancient landmarks which your fathers set.
Remember your ancestors' laws and have no regret.

#5 Honor

Do you see a man skilled in work? He stands before kings.
He will serve them and be known; a great honor he brings.

PROVERBS 23
More Wise Sayings

#6 Eating

When you sit to dine with a prince or king,
Note well what you see, the food that they bring.

Do not be given to gluttony's sin.
A knife to your throat will help discipline.

Do not want or crave this deceptive food.
His delicacies are evil and shrewd.

 # 7 Riches

Do not overdo or wear yourself out
Just to become rich; "Restraint!" you should shout.

Cast but a small glance on riches. Walk on!
They will sprout wings, and like eagles, they're gone.

 # 8 Bad Influences

Do not eat the food of a stingy man.
Also, do not crave anything he'll plan.

For he is the kind who thinks of the cost.
"Eat and drink," he says, but his heart is lost.

You will vomit up the little you ate
And will have wasted compliments you state.

9 Wisdom Abandoned

Don't speak to a fool for he plans to scorn
Your words of wisdom, abandoned, forlorn.

10 Orphans

Do not change or move an aged boundary stone
Or invade the fields of one who's alone.

For their defender is mighty and strong,
Protects the orphan, and corrects what's wrong.

11 Instruction

Now apply your heart to instruction's aim
And your ears to words that wisdom can claim.

12 Discipline

Do not withhold the training of a child.
Discipline must show love that makes him mild.

If you punish him with the rod and love,
He will never die, a blessing from above.

13 *Wisdom*

If your heart is wise and you speak what's right,
My heart will be glad, my son, my delight.

#14 *Fear of God*

Do not let your heart envy men who sin
But fear the Lord God; abide in discipline.

There is a future and a hope for you;
It won't be cut off if you will stay true.

#15 *Gluttony*

Listen to me, son; be wise with your heart.
Keep on the right path and never depart.

Do not join with those who drink too much wine
Or eat too much meat, thinking it is fine.

For drunkards, gluttons, and those men who lag
Are poor and lazy, and their clothes are rags.

16 *Parent's Joy*

Hear, pay attention to your father's words
Because he gave life and his love is heard.

Do not despise your mother when she's old.
She took care of you and all the household.

Always buy the truth and do not sell it.
Get wisdom's insight and to God commit.

A good man's father will greatly rejoice.
His son's righteousness shows every right choice.

Mothers and fathers find comfort and joy
When they see wisdom in their girl or boy.

17 Warning!

My son, look to me and give me your heart.
Always see my ways, never to depart.

For a prostitute is a pit. Don't dwell!
And a wayward wife is a narrow well.

She will lie in wait for unfaithful men
And will multiply these victims again.

18 Pitfalls of Drinking

Who has woe and gloom? Who has sorrow too?
Strife, complaints, trouble? Wounds without a clue?

Who has bloodshot eyes? Those who linger long
Over wine or drink. They're searching to belong.

Do not gaze at wine when it is bright red,
When it sparkles bright in the cup outspread.

When it swirls smoothly, be aware, watch out.
It bites like a snake, poison all about.

Your eyes see strange sights, your mind, always dazed.
Your heart imagines, confused and amazed.

You will be like one who on high seas sleeps.
He lies atop the mast, sowing what he reaps.

"They hit me," you say, "But I am not hurt,
And when I wake up, 'More drink,' I will blurt."

Wise Sayings

FOLLOW AND FEAR THE LORD GOD.

Wise Sayings Continued

19 The Envious Man

Do not envy wicked men; their company don't desire,
For their hearts plot violence, and trouble their lips inspire.

20 The Strong House

By wisdom, a house is built; through understanding, it's made.
By knowledge, the rooms are filled with rare treasures all arrayed.

#21 The Adviser

A wise man has great power. His knowledge increases might.
Waging his war needs guidance, good advisers for the fight.

#22 The Fool

Wisdom is not for the fool when assembled at the gate.
He does not open his mouth; he has nothing to debate.

#23 The Schemer

He who plots to do evil is a schemer; he deceives.
His ways of folly are sin. Men detest the webs he weaves.

#24 The Failure

If you falter in the day of suffering and trouble,
How small is your inner strength; you fail and become rubble.

#25 The Deliverer

Deliver those being led toward darkness and their death.
Hold back those stumbling toward slaughter and their last breath.

Do not say, "We did not know." He who weighs the heart sees you.
He who guards your life knows all. He'll repay the deeds you do.

#26 The Hope of Wisdom

Come and eat honey, my son, for it will taste very sweet.
Honey from the comb is good. Like wisdom, it is a treat.

Know, too, that wisdom is sweet, dear to your body and soul.
If you find it, there is hope that will be your lifelong goal.

#27 The Righteous

Do not lie in wait against a righteous man's dwelling place.
Do not rob or raid his house; you will be held in disgrace.

Even though the righteous fall, they'll fail seven times yet rise.
But the wicked are brought down by tragedy. Hear their cries.

#28 The Humble

Do not gloat or celebrate when your enemy stumbles.
When he falls down, don't rejoice, but let your heart be humble.

#29 The Judge

The Lord will see your response; He'll disapprove of your pride.
All His wrath now turns away. God will judge; He will decide.

#30 The Fear of the Lord

Do not fret because of men, those who slip down evil's slope.
Don't be envious of them for they have no future hope.

The lamp of all the wicked will be snuffed out in the dark.
Follow and fear the Lord God. His light and truth will embark.

Do not join the rebellious but fear the Lord and the king.
They'll send sudden destruction; calamity they will bring.

More to Learn

Further sayings of the wise: partiality is bad.
When judging other people, do not take away or add.

He who says to the guilty, "You're righteous and innocent,"
Will be cursed by the people. Nations will show discontent.

But it will go well with those who convict the guilty men.
Rich blessings will come to him who is a good citizen.

An honest and right answer is like a kiss on the lips.
It overflows with wisdom and with righteousness equips.

Finish all your outdoor work. Make it ready in the field,
And afterward, build your house, then good harvest soon will yield.

Do not speak or testify opposing your neighbor's word.
Without a cause or reason, deceiving him is absurd.

Do not say, "I'll do to him just as he has done to me.
I'll surely pay that man back for his deeds. Just wait and see."

I went past a sluggard's field, past the vineyard of the man
Who lacks judgment and wisdom. Thorns came up and overran.

The stone wall was in ruins; the ground was covered with weeds,
I applied my heart to see that a lesson met my needs.

This is the lesson I learned: a little sleep and slumber,
A little folding of the hands, causes debt in great number.

Poverty will come on you like a bandit; he will steal.
Famine, like a man who's armed, will come and take your last meal.

PROVERBS 25
More Proverbs of Solomon

These are more proverbs of Solomon, the great king,
Copied by the men under Hezekiah's wing.

Right Words, Right Time

It is God's right to conceal any concern,
But a king's glory is to search out facts and learn.

As heaven is high and the earth is far below,
So the hearts of kings are hidden, never to know.

Remove all the waste from the silver; purify,
Then the silversmith's fine vessel will satisfy.

Remove the wicked from the king's presence and throne;
Then the land will be pure, and righteousness will be known.

Don't exalt yourself in the king's presence or sight.
Do not claim a place among great men of might.

It's better for him to say to you, "Come up here,"
Than for him to cause humiliation and fear.

What your eyes have seen, do not bring hastily to court
For what will you do if neighbors shame your report?

If you fight your case with a neighbor and argue,
Do not betray him whose confidence is in you.

Lest he who hears it may expose your shame and guilt
For then you will lose the reputation you built.

A word well-spoken is like apples made of gold.
Gold set in silver is like treasures that are told.

Like a gold earring is a wise man's reprimand.
To listening ears, it's like a gem in his hand.

Like the cold of snow in time of harvest season
Is a messenger who you can trust with reason.

Those men who send him are refreshed in the spirit.
His masters rejoice as their ears love to hear it.

Like dark clouds and wind that do not bring any rain
Is a man who boasts of gifts he will never bring.

Through endless patience, a ruler is persuaded
For a gentle tongue can break a bone, unaided.

Self-Control

If you find honey, eat just enough, or you'll see
Too much sweetness, and sick to your stomach you'll be.

Seldom set foot in your neighbor's house that's well-known
For too much bother, and you will be left alone.

Like a club or sword is the man who has false words;
Like sharp arrows, his testimony is absurd.

Like a tooth that hurts or a lame foot that stumbles
Is reliance on the unfaithful who grumbles.

Singing happy songs to a heavy, downcast heart
Is like vinegar on soda, useless to start.

Or like a warm coat taken off on a cold day,
Not what you should do, so watch what you say.

If your enemy is hungry, give him some bread.
If he is thirsty, give him water as you're led.

In doing these deeds, you will heap up burning coals
On his wicked head; then the Lord rewards your soul.

As a strong north wind brings rain and powerful storms
So a cunning tongue will bring anger that transforms.

It's better to live on a roof, in the corner,
Than to share a house with a wife who's a scorner.

Like cold water to a soul that's tired and weary
Is good news from a land that's far and dreary.

Like a muddied spring that is polluted and grey
Is a righteous man who to the wicked, gives way.

It's not good to eat too much honey; it's so sweet,
And neither is it good to seek honor's conceit.

Like a city's walls that are crushed and broken down
Is a sinful man without self-control; he'll drown.

Solomon's
Proverbs Continued

LIKE SNOW IN SUMMER...

Solomon's Proverbs Continued

All About Fools

Like snow in summer or harvest in rain,
Honor for a fool, he'll never attain.

Like a fluttering sparrow's weary quest,
An undeserved curse will not come to rest.

A whip for a horse or halters for mules
Are much like a rod for the backs of fools.

Don't answer a fool, or soon you will see
You will be like him, and all will agree.

But answer a fool, his folly expose.
You will bring hope when you show you oppose.

He who sends a note by a foolish man
Cuts off his own feet and spoils his plan.

Like a lame man's leg that hangs limp and weak
Is a good proverb when foolish lips speak.

Like tying a stone in a sling to throw
Is giving honor to a fool or foe.

Like a sharp thorn bush in a drunkard's hand
Is a proverb that a fool can command.

Like a shrewd archer who shoots wild and is sly,
So is he who hires fools or a passer-by.

As a dog returns, his vomit to view,
So a fool repeats his folly anew.

Do you see a man wise in his own eyes?
A fool has more hope, we all realize.

The lazy person says, "Look up ahead!
A lion's in the road. I'll go back to bed."

A door on hinges opens and closes
Like a lazy man on his bed dozes.

The sluggard buries his hand in the dish.
He is too lazy to eat what he'll wish.

He now sees himself wiser than many;
His conceit is shown, and pride is plenty.

Handling Conflicts

Like one who seizes a dog by the ears
Is a passer-by who listens and hears.

He hears a quarrel, not even his own.
He wants to meddle; just leave it alone.

Like a crazed madman who shoots his arrows,
He deceives his neighbor, causing sorrows.

With firebrands of death, his neighbor believes.
"I'm only joking," he says as he leaves.

Without logs or wood, there will be no fire.
Without a gossip, a quarrel will tire.

As wood is to fire and charcoal to coal,
Being quarrelsome burns out of control.

Words of a gossip are like a choice bite.
They go down to man's inmost parts, his plight.

Like a glaze coating over a dull cup,
So are praising lips, but evil shows up.

Handling Liars

A malicious man likes to use disguise;
His lips sound true, but evil, his heart cries.

Though his speech will charm, do not believe him.
Hate and evil fill his heart to the brim.

His malice may be concealed, not disclosed,
But his wickedness will soon be exposed.

If a man digs a pit, he will fall inside.
If man rolls a stone, on him it will slide.

A lying tongue hates those people it hurts.
A flattering mouth works ruin, subverts.

PROVERBS 27
All About Life

Man's Pride

Don't boast of tomorrow for you do not know
What a day may bring, what God may bestow.

Let another praise you and not your own lips;
But other men's words, take heed to these tips.

Man's Evil Hand

Stones and rocks are heavy; sand can burden too,
But insults by fools weigh more; that is true.

Anger is so cruel, and fury is vast,
But who can stand when jealousy is cast?

Better hearing rebuke that's open and clear
Than hidden, masked love that will not appear.

Wounds from a loyal friend, you will learn to trust,
But an enemy deceives with disgust.

He who is full dislikes honey for a treat,
But to the hungry, what's bitter tastes sweet.

Like a bird that will stray from its little nest
Is a man who strays from his home that's blessed.

Man's Friends and Neighbors

Perfume and sweet incense bring joy to the heart,
So a friend's counsel is good to impart.

Do not forsake a friend, your dad's or your own.
Friends are a treasure whose value is known.

Don't go to your brother who lives far away
When you must have help and you can't delay.

Better a close neighbor who can lend a hand
When disaster strikes and your needs demand.

Man's Family

Be wise, my son, and bring delight to my heart;
Then I can answer scorn that others impart.

The prudent sees danger, and refuge he'll take,
But the fool keeps on to suffer and ache.

Do not lend your money to just any one;
Your own property will be held, my son.

He who loudly blesses his neighbor or friend
Early in the morning, curses it will send.

A quarrelsome wife is like a fast drip,
Constant, like the day when rain's in its grip.

Trying to control her is like stopping wind
Or holding oil; you cannot depend.

Man's Good Counsel

As iron sharpens iron, so a man can help you;
Sharpening others, excellence pursue.

He who tends a fig tree will eat of its fruit.
Care for a master brings honor's recruit.

As water will reflect a man's face, so true,
So will a man's heart reflect his virtue.

Neither death nor destruction can be satisfied;
Neither can man's eyes be content and abide.

The cauldron for silver, the furnace for gold,
But man is tested by the praise that he's told.

Though you grind up a fool like grinding grains,
Using pestle and mortar, folly remains.

Man as Provider

Diligently watch your flocks; their conditions know.
Attend to their needs so your herds will grow.

For riches do not last nor a crown secure
For generations can never be sure.

When hay is stored away, new growth will appear;
Then grass from the hills is gathered each year.

The lambs will provide wool; good clothing they yield.
The goats bring profit to buy a new field.

You will then have plenty of goats' milk to drink,
Food for your family; sustained, don't you think?

Moral Contrasts

WALK FROM DARKNESS TO LIGHT.

Moral Contrasts

Moral Truths

The wicked man will flee, though no one's in pursuit,
But every righteous man has boldness to impute.

When a country rebels, it will have many kings,
But a man of knowledge keeps order of all things.

A ruler oppresses the needy and the weak.
He is like driving rain that ruins crops; it's bleak.

Those who forsake the law will praise wicked men,
But those who keep the law obey and resist sin.

Evil men do not grasp fair justice in their land,
But those who seek the Lord fully have it in hand.

Moral Consequences

Better a man who's poor, who walks a blameless path,
Than a man who is rich with perverse ways of wrath.

A son who obeys the law knows discernment's place,
But a friend of gluttons sees his father's disgrace.

He who increases wealth by interest that's steep
Will soon see it given to the poor, the lost sheep.

If anyone rejects the law and turns away,
Even his prayers to God are abhorred every day.

He who leads the upright along an evil path
Will fall into a trap of his own evil wrath.

But the blameless and pure will receive a great gift,
One of inheritance, and our God will uplift.

A rich man may be wise in his own eyes and ways,
But a poor man who sees through him will be amazed.

When the righteous triumph, elation soon will come,
But when evil rises, men will hide and succumb.

Moral Confessions

He who conceals his sins will soon see poverty,
But all who will confess find that mercy sets free.

Blessed is the man who fears and honors the Lord God,
But he whose heart is hard finds trouble with each nod.

Moral Judgments

Like a roaring lion or the charge of a bear
Is the rule of a man that causes great despair.

An oppressive leader lacks judgment, causing strife,
But he who hates all greed will enjoy a long life.

A man that's tormented by murder's guilt and shame
Will be a fugitive until death all will blame.

He whose walk is blameless is kept secure by all,
But he whose ways are mean suddenly sees his fall.

He who cares for his land will have abundant food,
But one who chases dreams, poverty will intrude.

A faithful, loyal man will soon be richly blessed,
But one who loves riches will always be distressed.

To show favoritism is harmful, never good,
Yet man will break laws just to have bread, if he could.

A stingy, selfish man desires a rich estate
And is so unaware that poverty awaits.

Moral Counsel

He who rebukes a man will hear more praises sung
Than a man who talks well with a flattering tongue.

If you cheat your parents and don't think it is wrong,
You are evil's partner and to destruction belong.

A greedy man stirs up dissention and trouble,
But he who trusts the Lord thrives and prospers double.

He who trusts in himself is foolish and absurd,
But walking in wisdom leads to safety ensured.

He who gives to the poor will have all that he needs,
But he who hides his eyes will have curses indeed.

When wicked men rise to power, the people hide,
But when the wicked die, the righteous live in pride.

PROVERBS 29
God is in Control

Decisions

A man who remains stiff-necked after rebukes' decree
Will suddenly be destroyed without a remedy.

When the righteous people thrive, they rejoice with delight.
When the wicked rule the land, the people groan with fright.

Any man who loves wisdom will bring his father joy,
But being with a harlot, his wealth he will destroy.

By a king's truth and justice, a country is stable,
But a king who is greedy, his bribes will disable.

One who flatters his neighbor is spreading a large net
For his feet will get caught up; his deception is set.

An evil man will be snared by his own deeds and sin,
But a good and righteous man can be happy within.

The righteous cherish justice for the poor and needy,
But the wicked do not care; no concern do we see.

Peace

Mockers stir up a city, but wise men turn away.
Any anger that erupts, they avoid every day.

If a wise man goes to court with a fool who shows rage,
He will never be at peace. Avoid this; don't engage.

Bloodthirsty men hate a man who values honesty.
They seek to kill the upright; their wickedness we see.

A fool declares his anger for everyone to hear,
But a wise man keeps control and his conscience clear.

Parents

The hard rod of correction will reveal wisdom's case,
But a child left to himself sees his mother's disgrace.

When wicked men thrive and shine, so does evil and sin,
But the righteous will then see their downfall; truth will win.

Fathers, discipline your son, and he will give you peace.
He will bring delight to you, your soul's comfort release.

Obedience

Where there is no revelation, people cast off restraint,
But blessed is he who obeys, keeps the law, and doesn't faint.

A servant cannot be changed; mere words will not correct.
Although he understands them, he will only reject.

Do you see a man who speaks in urgency, in haste?
There is more hope for a fool than for him; he's disgraced.

If a man pampers the needs of his servant from youth,
He will bring grief in the end. Be mindful of this truth.

An angry man will stir up dissension filled with strife,
And a hot-tempered one will commit sins all his life.

Humility and Trust

A man's pride will bring him low; it's his enemy within,
But a man's humble spirit gains honor; he will win.

The accomplice of a thief is his own enemy.
He is put under an oath. Testify? Don't agree.

Fear of man will only prove to be a trap, a snare,
But all who trust in the Lord are kept safe in His care.

Many seek an audience with a ruler in fear,
But it's only from the Lord that justice will appear.

The righteous ones will detest dishonest men who lie.
The wicked, also, will hate the upright who comply.

The Sayings of Agur

WALK WITH DIGNITY.

PROVERBS 30

The Sayings of Agur

Confession of Faith

I'm an ignorant man. Understanding? I've none.
I know neither of wisdom nor of the Holy One.

Who has gone to heaven and then returned so grand?
Who has gathered the wind and held it in His hand?

Who has wrapped the waters in His garment, His cloak?
Who has now established the earth with words He spoke?

What is His holy name and the name of His Son?
Tell me if you know this! Is He the Mighty One?

Every one of God's words is flawless, absolute.
He is a shield to all when they are destitute.

Do not add to His word, or He will rebuke you.
He'll prove you a liar with the words you construe.

A Prayer

Two things I ask of You, Lord; do not refuse me.
Before I die and leave, grant these requests, I plea.

Keep all falsehood and lies far away and apart.
Give me neither riches nor poverty impart,

But give me only bread; my daily needs be met.
Otherwise, I may have too much and be in debt.

I'll then be heard to say, "Who is the Lord above?'
Or I may become poor and steal things I love.

Caution

Don't slander a servant, to his master transmit,
Or he'll come to curse you, and you will pay for it.

Wicked Generations

There's a generation that curses their father
And will not bless mothers, too selfish to bother.

Those who are pure and true in their own eyes and mind
Are not yet cleansed of sin. Their filth has made them blind.

Those whose eyes are haughty, so arrogant with pride,
Whose glances are scornful, yet their hearts are sad inside.

Those whose teeth are swords, whose jaws are set with knives,
Devour the poor on earth. They must run for their lives.

Never Satisfied

The leech has two daughters. "Give! Give!" they always cry.
They never say, "Enough!" Nothing will satisfy.

Never to satisfy! These four things, it is true:
The grave, the barren womb, desert land, and fire too.

Eyes that mock a father and his mother despise,
Ravens and vultures soon pick out and eat his eyes.

Amazing Things

Three things are amazing. I don't understand four.
The way of an eagle in the sky, he will soar.

The way of a snake as he crawls upon a rock,
The way that a ship sails from the seas to a dock,

And the way of a man who falls deeply in love
With a girl of his dreams, a blessing from above.

Intolerable Things

An adulteress sins; this is her way and her song.
She eats, and then she says, "I have done nothing wrong."

The earth shakes and trembles under three things or four.
It can't bear up with these. It can't take any more.

A servant who is king, becoming a success;
A fool who's full of food and prospers to impress;

A woman who is married and is harsh, a disgrace;
A maid servant who's above her mistress' place.

Wise but Small

Four things on earth are small, yet they are very wise.
Ants, who have little strength, yet store food of great size.

Badgers are weak creatures; they are little in might,
Yet they will make their homes in high rocks, without fright.

The locusts have no king, yet they advance in rank.
Lizards, easily caught, yet in palaces they slank.

Walk with Dignity

There are three stately things in their stride and walk,
Four that move with dignity as they pursue and stalk:

A lion, so mighty among every beast,
Who will never retreat but on enemies feast;

A tall strutting rooster; a goat, proud in his pen;
A king with his army standing tall with his men.

Keep Calm and Quiet

If you have been foolish, exalting your own life,
If you have planned evil, cover your mouth in strife.

As milk creates butter when you labor and churn,
As hurt noses will bleed, so your strife brings concern.

The Sayings of King Lemuel

Leaders, Speak Out for Justice

The words of King Lemuel, which his mother taught;
These oracles and truths to her son, she brought.

O my son of my womb and son of each vow,
Don't spend time on women or ruin allow.

It's not for kings, Lemuel, to drink beer or wine,
Lest they drink and forget the law's great design.

Give beer to the dying and wine to those who grieve.
Let them drink and forget, their sorrows relieve.

Speak up for the silent, for the poor, and what's right.
Speak up and judge fairly and for justice, fight.

The Ideal Wife

A wife of good character, can anyone find?
She is worth more than rubies. She's gentle and kind.

Her husband has trust in her. She meets all his needs.
All her life, she brings him favor and kind deeds.

She can select wool and flax and works with eager hands.
She is like the merchant ships; brings food from far lands.

She gets up while it's still dark to provide good food
For family and servants. She's never gruff or rude.

She will consider a field and then will buy it.
She will plant a good vineyard; all will benefit.

She sets about her hard work with vigor and might.
Her arms are strong for each task. Work is her delight.

Everything she makes is good. Each profit is won.
Her lamp keeps burning at night; her work is never done.

She uses a spinning wheel and holds the spindle.
She makes her own wool and flax, gets wood for kindle.

She reaches out to the poor and to the needy.
Her hands always extend out; she's never greedy.

When it snows, she has no fear for those in her care
For all of them are clothed in scarlet that's so rare.

She makes covers for her beds and makes for herself
Clothes in fine purple linen, filling up each shelf.

Her husband is respected at the city gate.
He sits there, among the elders, to advocate.

She makes fine linen garments; they're ready to sell.
She supplies merchant sashes; she does very well.

She is clothed with a calm strength and with dignity.
She can laugh at days to come, smiling visibly.

She speaks with lots of wisdom, instruction that's true.
Faithfulness is on her tongue. Knowledge she'll pursue.

She watches over the affairs of all her household.
She doesn't eat the bread of idleness, we're told.

Her children rise up to call her blessed and adored.
Her husband praises her. All their love is outpoured.

Many women will work hard and do noble things,
But you surpass all of them. Your faithful deeds sing.

Charm is very deceptive. Beauty doesn't last.
But a woman who fears the Lord has praises so vast.

Give her the rewards she's earned. Let her works bring praise.
Exclaim at the city gate, "Honor her all her days."

CPSIA information can be obtained
at www.ICGtesting.com
Printed in the USA
LVHW012146310720
662077LV00011B/622